Hannelore Wernhard

The Knitted Farmyard

Translated by
Hilary Simpson

Edited,
and with drawings, by
Jan Messent

SEARCH PRESS

Introduction

The knitted farmyard is created out of a mixture of knitting and crochet, although all the main pieces are knitted. The base is the size of a small rug, and would be ideal for a child's room, especially with the family figures and farm-animals which live on it in their buildings. Although it is quite a large task to make everything on the farm, the quantities of materials needed are quite small. Oddments of knitting yarns, rug-canvas and embroidery threads, terylene padding and pipe-cleaners are the main components.

SIZES, TENSIONS AND MATERIALS

The sizes of the various farmyard pieces will depend partly on the kinds of yarn you use and your personal tension in knitting. Try to use whatever yarns you have to hand; the figures and animals in the patterns described were made in a fine 3-ply and using size 2¼mm., 2¾mm., and 3mm. needles. (These correspond to old sizes 13, 12 and 11 respectively.)

PATTERN ALTERATIONS

This English version of this knitted farmyard has undergone a few slight changes from the original German in order to make some articles easier to knit and to change the dog from crochet to knitting. You may find therefore that the article you have made looks a little different in some respects from the photograph although in essence it will be the same. There is plenty of scope for individual touches, changes of colour and extra accessories: add or subtract anything to make your own farmyard unique.

STITCHES

The main stitches used are garter stitch (i.e. every row is knitted), which is abbreviated as g.s., and Stocking stitch (i.e. alternate rows of knit and purl), which is abbreviated as s.s. Other abbreviations are as follows:

k – knit	k 2 tog. – knit 2 together
p – purl	beg. – beginning
sts – stitches	rem. – remaining
ch. – chain	cm. – centimetres
dec. – decrease	mm. – millimetres
inc. – increase	in. – inches

Note. As you work, check that your knitted pieces will fit the areas they are being made for, particularly the clothes, as your knitting may have to be adjusted by one or two rows or stitches here and there.

Adult figures

The Materials required are:

6 pipe-cleaners for each figure

Terylene wadding (about ½ metre should be enough for all the figures and animals).

Thick pink yarn for binding.

Fine 3-ply skin-coloured yarn for knitted body-coverings. (A 25gm. ball will be enough for all the adults and children.) One pair each 2¼mm. and 2¾mm. needles, wool needles, and scissors and tape-measure.

THE BASIC BODY-SHAPE

The following instructions are for all the figures; the sizes for the children are given in Fig. 7.

Take two pipe-cleaners and lay them end to end overlapping by about ¾in. (2cm.). Twist them together where they overlap, to make one long piece (see Fig. 1). Now do the same with two more, and lay the two pieces side by side. Bend into shape as shown, to make the head (see Fig. 2). Twist the legs gently together and turn the feet up very slightly to make the legs even. Take two more pipe-cleaners and lay them evenly across the shoulders, twisting them as shown. Turn up the end slightly to shorten the arms (see Fig. 3).

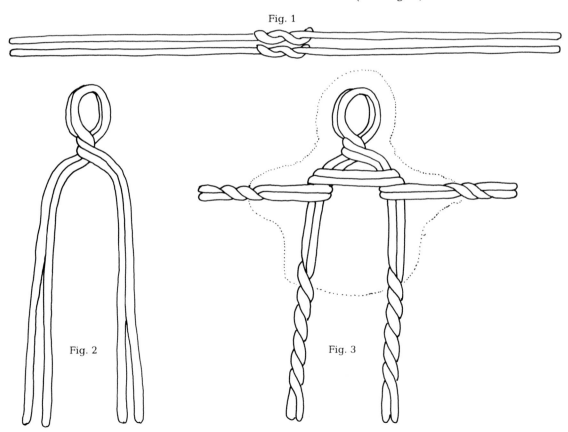

Fig. 1

Fig. 2

Fig. 3

Figs. 1–3. The pipe-cleaner framework for the figures.

The mother and father, two children and baby, and dog

The little boy and the ducks

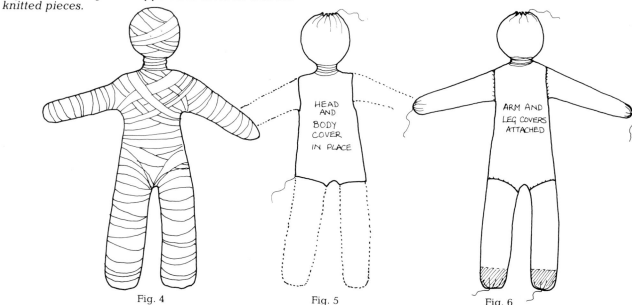

Figs. 4–6. The figure wrapped and covered with the knitted pieces.

HEAD
AND
BODY
COVER
IN PLACE

ARM AND
LEG COVERS
ATTACHED

Fig. 4   Fig. 5   Fig. 6

Cover the head and body with a piece of padding, and bind this gently in place with the thick pink yarn, winding it also around the legs and arms to thicken them. Draw the yarn tightly around the neck to define it (see Fig. 4).

Knitted covers for adult figures

(*Note*. The farmer's wife is made differently, see page 11). Use the 2¼mm. needles and the fine skin-coloured yarn. Begin with the main body-piece which also covers the head. Cast on 22sts and work in s.s. for 16 rows from the top of the legs to the under-arm. This should now be checked against the figure framework as sizes will vary depending on yarn, tension and the padding on the body. Now divide for the arms. K 6. Turn and work on these 6sts, alone for 6 more rows. Break off the yarn. Attach the yarn to the other group of sts and k 10. Work on these 10sts alone for 6 more rows. Break off yarn. Attach the yarn to the last group and work 6 more rows, but do not break the yarn. Now continue across all the sts for 13 more rows. (Again, this should be checked

against the figure, bearing in mind that the knitting will stretch a little).

Do not cast off; gather the sts on to a threaded wool-needle and draw them together. Slip the arms into the holes, and the last sts on top of the head. Sew up the back seam, wrapping the yarn tightly around the neck. At the base, pull the two edges together in the centre between the legs, ready for the leg-pieces to be joined on (see Fig. 5).

The arms

Cast on 10sts and work 18 rows in s.s. Check to see whether this piece fits the arms on your figure. K 2 tog. all along the next row, then thread the yarn on to the last 5sts and gather up. Slip this on to the arm with the gathers at the hand end, and sew up. Attach the piece around the arm-hole, and make another piece to match.

The legs

Cast on 10sts and work in s.s. for the length of the leg as far as the ankle – about 22 rows. If the legs are not as long as you would like them to be, take this opportunity to add more rows at this point and pad the shoe area with wool before sewing up.

The last 6 rows are worked in shoe-colour in either s.s. or g.s. They are finished off in the same way as the hands (the farmer wears separately-made boots). Sew the cast-on edge to the bottom of the body-covering around the top of the leg.

Make another in the same way (see Fig. 6).

The hair and beards are embroidered using scraps of brown and fair wool, and the spectacles are made of brass wire.

ADULTS' CLOTHES

Trousers

Knitted in g.s. on size 2¼mm. needles in fine 3-ply or 4-ply. Cast on 22sts and knit 26 rows.
Row 27; Cast off 12sts and k to end of row. (10sts).
Row 28; K 10, turn and cast on 12sts. K to end of row (22sts).
Knit across all sts for 25 more rows. Cast off.

Fold the two side edges towards each other and sew up the centre back seam. Now sew up the inside leg seams (see Fig. 8). The farmer's trousers have a pair of braces made of crochet chain.

Fig. 8. The trouser pattern.

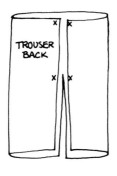

Fig. 8

Father's shirt (see page 4)

The back and front are worked in one piece, with separate sleeves. Use size 2¾mm. needles, cast on 12sts and work 16 rows in s.s.
Next row; k 3, cast off 6sts, k to end.
Next row; p 3, turn and cast on 3sts. K back to the beg. of the row, working into the back of the 4th st. Work 5 more rows on these 6sts. ending on a p row. Break off yarn and attach it to the other 3sts, casting on 3 more sts at the same time on the neck edge.

Purl back to the end of the row, working into the back of the 4th st. Work 5 rows on these 6sts ending with a k row, then work across the other 6sts also, to join the two sides.
Next row; p. Work 8 more rows and cast off.

Fig. 7. Body measurements after covering. These may vary a little, depending on the yarn etc.

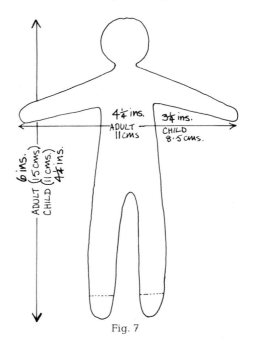

Fig. 7

The farmer's wife and her mule

The farmer and his donkey

Sleeves

Cast on 15sts and work 2 rows in s.s.
Cast off 2sts at beg. of next 2 rows.
Next row; k 2 tog, k 7, k 2 tog, (9sts). Cast off p-wise.
Make another one the same. Lay the shirt body section out flat and sew the sleeve, centrally positioned, to this. Then sew the under-arm and side seams all at once. You may wish to work a row of crochet around the neck to finish it off. The back opening may be stitched up once it is on the figure but to make it easy to remove, you may prefer to attach a tiny button and loop.

Sleeve for child's version

Cast on 12sts and work 2 rows in s.s.
Cast off 2sts at beg. of next 2 rows.
Next row; k 2 tog, k 4, k 2 tog. (6sts). Cast off p-wise.

Farmer's shirt and mother's pullover (see pages 4 and 9)

This is made in one piece from one sleeve edge to the other. It opens down the back from neck to hem (see Fig. 9).
Use 2¾mm. needles and 3-ply or 4-ply yarn.
Cast on 16sts and work 12 rows in s.s.
Cast on 8 more sts at beg. of the next 2 rows, working into the back of the 9th st. on each row (32sts). Work 4 more rows, then divide for the neck opening as follows:
K 15, cast off 2sts, k to end of row.
Work 3 rows on these 15sts.
Next row; * k 2, yarn forward, k 2 tog, * 3 times. K 3. This makes 3 buttonholes.
Next row; p, then cast off.
Rejoin the yarn to the other sts and work 8 rows, beg. with a p row.
Next row; cast on 17sts p back across all 32sts, purling into the back of the 18th st.
Work 5 more rows, ending with a p row.
Cast off 8sts at beg. of the next 2 rows, and work 12 rows in s.s.
Next row; cast off.
Attach 3 tiny buttons to the back opening, and sew up the seams.

Fig. 9

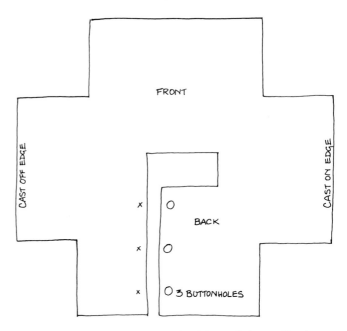

Fig. 9. Diagram of the farmer's shirt and the mother's pullover.

THE FARMER (see page 9)

The same shirt pattern is used as for the mother's pullover, though the colour is different. The trousers are also the same, except that the farmer's have crocheted straps, or braces. His hat may be knitted or crocheted: here is the knitted version.

Hat

Use 3-ply yarn and size 2¼mm. needles: cast on 22sts.
Work 4 rows in s.s., then k 2 tog. all along the row.
Purl the next row, then gather the rem. sts on to a thread and leave. With the right side facing you, pick up 22sts from the cast-on edge and k back, inc. into every st.
K 2 rows and then cast off. Sew up the back seam, and make a crochet chain to go around the brim.

Boots

Use 2¼mm. needles and dark-brown 3-ply yarn. Cast on 15sts and work 10 rows in s.s. Row 11; p, then work in reversed s.s. for 6 more rows. Next row; k 2 tog. all along the row to the last st., k 1. Gather up the rem. sts on to a length of yarn and sew up. Place a small amount of padding in the toe of the boot and fix on to the foot.

THE FARMER'S WIFE (see pages 8 and 21)

The farmer's wife wears a long skirt which is enclosed at the base with an oval-shaped piece of card, so her legs do not need a knitted covering. Unlike the other figures, her clothes are not removable; her dress-bodice and head-covering are made in one piece, as are the sleeves and hands.

Bodice and head-covering

Use size 2¼mm. needles and dress-coloured yarn. Cast on 22sts and work in s.s. for 4 rows. Then divide for the arms: k 6, turn, and work on these 6sts for 6 more rows. Cut the yarn and attach it to the other group of sts.
K 10, turn and work on these 10sts for 6 more rows. Complete as for first section.
Work 6 rows on the next 6sts, then p across all 22sts. Work 4 more rows to finish the neckline.
Change to the skin-coloured yarn, and work in s.s. for 11 rows. Finish the top of the head as for the other figures.

Sleeves and hands

These are worked in g.s. and s.s. respectively. Using dress-coloured yarn, cast on 10sts and k 16 rows.
Change to skin-coloured yarn and s.s. Work 4 more rows.
On the 5th row, k 2 tog. 5 times.
Gather the rem. sts on to a thread and sew the hand and arm seam on the wrong side. Reverse the sleeve and attach to the figure.

Skirt

Use size 3mm. needles and dress-coloured yarn, cast on 25sts and work in g.s. for 16cm. Cast off and sew this edge to the cast-on edge. Gather one edge of the tube and attach it to the bodice. Cut an oval-shaped card for the base of the skirt and stick it in place inside the hem to give a firm base to the figure.

Apron

Use size 2mm. needles, pale yarn, 14sts, 4 rows g.s., then 22 rows s.s. Cast off. Gather the top slightly and sew on to the figure. Crochet a long chain about 8in. (20cm.), and sew this around the waistline to tie at the back.

Hair

Cut 6 × 8¾in. (15 × 22cm.) lengths of coppery-red yarn and sew these centrally to the middle of the head. Then tie them together at the nape of the neck, securing them there with a few sts. Tie them again further down and sew on to the middle of the head at the top, twisting them into a knot and sewing them down firmly. Embroider the features as shown.

THE CHILDREN (see page 4)

The children are made in the same way as the adults except that the pipe-cleaner frame will be shortened at the hands and feet (see the measurements given in Fig. 7). The body-covering is also made in the same way, but here you should check the length of each piece against the child's figure before finishing. You may also find that you need one or two less sts than the adult pattern. The little girl wears white ankle socks which should be knitted into the bottom of the legs before the shoes. The hair of both children is embroidered on to the head in fair and dark yarns; the little girl may have plaits.

Trousers

These are worked as for the adults (see Fig. 8) except that they are shorter. Use size 2¼mm. needles, cast on 12sts and, to divide for the legs, cast off half the stitches.

The children and their pony, not to mention the dog

The sheep are grazing by the shed

The jumpers

The boy's jumper is knitted in stripes but the instructions are the same as for the father's shirt except for the sleeves. A smaller version of these is to be found at the end of that pattern. Each piece should be measured for length against the figure. The girl's jumper is a sleeveless version of the same pattern.

THE BABY (see page 4)

The same kind of wire construction is used as for the other figures, but on a much smaller scale. Only three pipe-cleaners are used for the frame, two for the head and body and one bent in half for the arms. Turn the feet and hands up so that the overall length is about 2⅜in. (6cm.) and the width across the arms is about 1¾in. (4.5cm.). There is no need to use padding on this small frame, only thick pink yarn to bind it round. The body-covering and rompers are made in one piece in s.s., beginning with the head.

Knitted cover and rompers

Use size 2¼mm. needles and fine pink yarn, cast on 12sts and work 8 rows. Change to blue yarn and work 2 rows. Now make holes for the arms as follows:
K 2, yarn forward, k 2 tog., k 4, yarn forward, k 2 tog., k 2.
Work across all sts making a total of 10 blue rows, then divide for the legs.
K 6 and work on these 6sts for 10 rows. Change to pink yarn and work 4 rows. Leave the sts on a thread. Work the other leg to match. Slip the arms through the two holes and sew up the leg and back seams. Now make the two arms: cast on 6sts in white yarn and work 4 rows. Purl the next row, then change to pink yarn and work 2 rows. Draw the thread through the rem. sts and complete as for other arms. Embroider features and a little hair if you wish.

The Animals

Begin with the simplest and smallest, and work towards the larger and more complicated animals.

HENS AND COCKERELS (see pages 1 and 24)

You will need small amounts of 3-ply or 4-ply yarn in brown, white and red, a very small amount of yellow for the beaks, and some brightly-coloured embroidery cottons for the cockerel's tail. For the hen's legs you will need half a pipe-cleaner each, and terylene wadding for the bodies. Use size 2¾mm. and 3mm. needles. All birds are knitted in g.s.:
Cast on 18sts in brown yarn and k 3 rows.
4th row; k 2 tog., then k to end of row.
Repeat row 4 until there are only 6sts left. Cast off.
Complete as shown in the diagram, making a crochet chain for the tail feathers. The cockerel's tail is larger and more brightly-coloured. Use the half pipe-cleaner to make the legs and wrap it round with yarn before stitching into place.

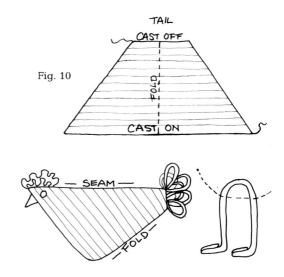

Fig. 10. The Hen. Basic shape, sewn shape and legs.

DUCKS (see page 5)

Cast on 22sts in white yarn and k 3 rows.
4th row; k 2 tog., k to end of row.
Repeat this row 11 more times.
Knit 9 more rows on the rem. 10sts. Cast off.
Fold the shape as shown, stuff, and finish off with beak and eyes.

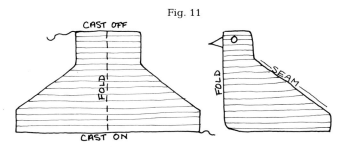

Fig. 11

Fig. 11. The Duck. Basic and sewn shape.

KITTEN (see pages 20 and 21)

You will need small oddments of 3-ply or 4-ply yarns in grey, white and black, or any cat-colour you wish. Size 2¾mm. or 3mm. needles. Cast on 8sts in body-colour and work in s.s.
Knit 1 row.
2nd row; inc. into every st. (16sts), then work 8 rows.
Row 11; k 2 tog. all along the row (8sts).
Work 6 rows then draw a thread through the sts, pad the shape and sew up. Gather a thread around the neck. Make a tail of 4sts and 10 rows in s.s.

Legs

Use size 2¼mm. needles, cast on 7sts with white yarn and work 9 rows s.s. Make 4.

Ears

Cast on 3sts with black yarn, k 2 rows and cast off.

PIG (see page 20)

You will need small amounts of pink or beige yarn. Note that in this version the legs are made separately from the body. Begin at the back and work towards the nose, using g.s. on size 2¾mm. or 3mm. needles.
Cast on 20sts and k 24 rows.
Now dec. on alternate rows as follows:
Row 25; k 7, k 2 tog., k 2, k 2 tog., k 7.
Row 27; k 6, k 2 tog., k 2, k 2 tog., k 6.
Row 29; k 5 and continue in the same manner as above.
Row 31; k 4 ditto.
Work 2 rows straight.
Row 34; k 2 tog. to the end of the row.
Row 35; p and then draw the last sts on to a thread, using this to sew up the body after padding it.

Legs

Use size 2mm. needles, cast on 8sts, and work 10 rows s.s.
Make 4. Embroider the eyes and make a curly tail of crochet.

SHEEP (see page 13)

For the body you will need white yarn (bouclé, or curly wool is best), and fawn or black yarn for the faces and legs. You will also need 2 pipe-cleaners for the legs. The body is knitted in g.s., and the faces and legs in s.s. You will also need terylene wadding, needle sizes 2¼mm. and 3mm., and yarn for the eyes.
For the body, begin at the tail-end, using white yarn and 3mm. needles, cast on 18sts and k 17 rows.
Dec. 1st. at the beg. and end of the next row, and also on rows 20 and 22.
Row 23; change to 2mm. needles and fawn or black yarn and work 8 rows in s.s. (this is the nose). Draw the rem. sts. on to a length of yarn, pad the cavity and sew it up with the seam underneath.

Legs

Take 2 pipe-cleaners and fold them in half. Now curve them round and insert one end into one side of

The farmer and his wife look out over their land from the village

the body and out at the other, through the knitting, where one pair of legs should be. Do the same for the other pair, then bend the wire up so that it is four-fold and half as long. The knitted leg-covering can now be slipped over these and sewn in place.

Using size 2¼mm. needle and fawn or black yarn, cast on 8sts and work 10 rows. Draw up the sts at the foot, and make 3 more pieces the same.

Ears

With 2mm. needles, white yarn, 3sts, 5 rows. Do not cast off. Draw sts up and sew on with rem. thread.

DOG (see pages 4, 12, 29 and 32)

Instead of being crocheted, as in the photograph, this version is knitted and the legs are made separately from the body. It will, however, look more or less the same as the one on the German farm.

You will need small amounts of white 3-ply or 4-ply yarn, and tan for the spots and ears, 4 pipe-cleaners for the frame, padding and a thick yarn for binding. Also, size 2¼mm. needles (see Fig. 12). Make the frame as shown in the diagram, noting that each piece of wire is a *double* pipe-cleaner. Pad it

lightly and bind this in place ready for the knitted cover (see Fig. 13).

Begin at the nose, and cast on 12sts.
Rows 1–6, s.s. Rows 7–12, g.s.
Inc. 1st. at beg. of the next 6 rows (18sts).
K 6 rows straight.
Inc. 1st. at beg. of next 2 rows (20sts).
K 16 rows straight.

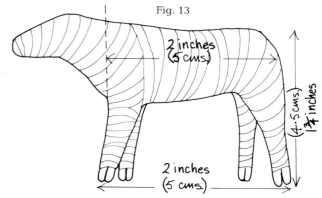

Fig. 13

Fig. 13. The dog after wrapping, with approximate measurements.

Last row; k 2 tog. to end of row, thread the length of yarn on to a needle and draw this through the 10sts. This is the dog's tail-end. Gather the cast-on edge on to the dog's nose and sew up as in the diagram (Fig. 14).

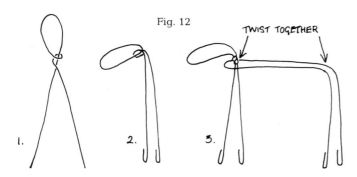

Fig. 12

TWIST TOGETHER

Fig. 12. The wire framework for the dog.

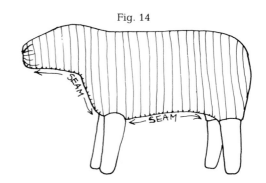

Fig. 14

Fig. 14. The dog, with body-cover in place.

Legs

6sts, 12 rows. Gather last sts on to a thread for the foot-end. Make 4.

Ears

In brown or tan yarn, 4sts, k 4 rows.
Last row, k 2 tog. twice, then cast off.

THE COW (see page 24)

This is worked in g.s. all through, except for the horns and the udder. In this version, the legs are made separately from the body. You will need small amounts of 3-ply or 4-ply yarn in beige, or any other cow-colour you choose, also oddments of pink and brown. Size 2¼mm. and 3mm. needles and padding. It will be found more convenient to attach the udder *before* the legs!
With size 3mm. needles, cast on 30sts and begin at the tail-end of the body. K 38 rows.
Row 39; k 2 tog., k 6, k 2 tog., k 10, k 2 tog., k 6, k 2 tog. (26sts)
Row 40; Knit. Row 41; dec. 1st at each end of row.
Repeat the last 2 rows until there are 18sts on the needle.
Row 48; k 12, turn and k 6. Work on the centre sts only – turn and k 5.
Turn and k 4.
Turn and k 2.
Turn and k 4.
Turn and k 6.
Turn and k to the end of the row.
Next row; dec. 1st. at both ends of the row (16sts).
K 10 more rows.
Last row; k 2 tog. to end of the row, and gather these 8sts on to a thread and draw up.

Legs

Using size 2¼mm. needles, cast on 12sts and work in g.s. for 22 rows. Gather these sts on to a thread and draw up to form the foot, then sew up the seam, pad firmly and attach the cast-on edge to the body. Make 3 more in the same way. *Note:* the legs will look different from those in the photograph.

Ears

2¼mm. needles, 5sts, 8 rows of g.s.
Row 9; k 2 tog., k 1, k 2 tog.
Row 10; k 2 tog., k 1. Cast off. Fold in half and attach to the head as shown in the picture.

Horns

Use paler yarn and 2¼mm. needles, working in s.s. Cast on 6sts, work 10 rows, then k 2 tog. 3 times. Draw the 3sts on to a thread and sew up. Pad slightly and attach as shown.

Udder

Pink 3-ply yarn, 2¼mm. needles, work in s.s. 16sts, 6 rows.
Gather all sts on to a thread and draw up, pad, and sew on.
Make 4 teats: 4sts, 4 rows of s.s. Draw sts on to thread.

Tail

Using double yarn, make a crochet chain 5cm. long, and fix a tassel to the end. Fix this high up on the cow's back.

PONY (see pages 12 and 25)

This is knitted all in one piece like a skin, beginning with the back legs and ending with the nose (Fig. 15). It is a little more complicated than any of the other patterns, so if you prefer a simpler version it is suggested that you use the cow (body and legs) pattern, and substitute the pony's ears, mane and tail. You will need 3-ply or 4-ply yarns for the main body-colour and small oddments for the mane and tail. Padding will also be needed as well as needles size 2¼mm. and 3mm., and an extra pair. Garter st. is used for all except the nose, and the hooves are made separately.
With the 3mm. needles, cast on 46sts and k 5 rows.
Next row; k 22, inc. into next 2sts., k 22 (48sts).
Knit 7 more rows.

*The farmer, his pigs, and the kitten, outside the barn (right)
and stable*

The farmer's wife accompanied by the kitten and the cockerel, picks lettuces. The stable and trees are in the background

Row 14; k 23, inc. into next 2sts, k 23 (50sts).
Row 15; k 8, turn and k 5 rows on these 8 sts with an extra needle. Cast these 8 sts off and break off the yarn.
Rejoin the yarn to the centre section and k to the end of the row. Row 17 as Row 15.
Row 18; rejoin yarn to centre section, cast on 3sts and knit to end of row.
Row 19; cast on 3sts, and k to end of row (40sts).
Knit 4 more rows.
Row 24; Inc. into first st., k 18, k 2 tog., k 18, inc. into last st. (42sts). Knit 7 more rows.
Row 32; k 2 tog., k 18, k 2 tog., k 17, k 2 tog. (39sts).
Knit 6 more rows.
Rows 39 and 40; cast off 3sts at beg., of these 2 rows (33sts).
Rows 41 and 42; cast on 8sts and k to end of row (49sts).
Knit 10 rows on these 49sts.
Row 53; k 8, turn and work 5 more rows on these 8sts. Cast off. Rejoin yarn to the centre section and k to end.
Row 55; as Row 53.
Rejoin yarn to centre section, cast on 3sts and k to end.
Row 57; Cast on 3sts and k to end (38sts).
Shape neck; k 7, turn and k back on these 7sts.
Next row; knit across all sts.
Repeat the last instructions 3 more times (i.e. twice at each side), then shape the top of the head.
K 23, turn, k 8, turn, k to end.
Next row; knit across all sts.
Repeat this procedure twice more. Shape nose as follows:
k 2 tog. all along the row. Now work 10 rows in s.s.
Next row; k 2 tog. all along the row, and gather the last sts on to a thread.

Ears

Use size 2¼mm. needle and work in s.s. Cast on 7sts and work 5 rows. Then dec. 1st. each end of the 6th and 8th rows.
Draw the rem. 3sts on to a thread and gather up.
Sew eyes and nostrils as shown, and cut lengths of contrasting yarn for the mane and tail.

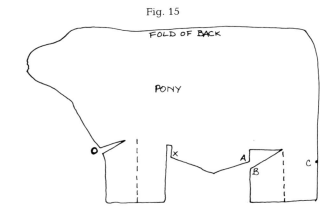

Fig. 15

Fig. 15. The shape of the pony-skin.

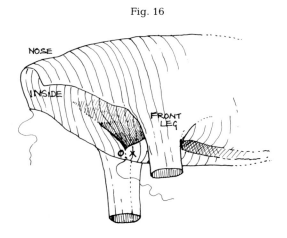

Fig. 16

Fig. 16. The front part of the pony-skin, showing the method of sewing the legs and under-seam.

Hooves (Make 4)

Cast on 12sts in black yarn, and work 4 rows in g.s., then draw up all sts on to yarn and sew up to make a cup shape.

Sew these on to the bottom of each leg.

Making up: run a gathering thread around the cast-on edge, then gather up to make a rounded tail-end. The padding of the 'pony-skin' is important to the success of the overall shape as it will tend to look very strange until the end of the process when its eyes, ears, hooves, mane and tail have been added. The diagram shows how to sew up the skin. Pad the legs before the body, and manipulate the padding gently to get a good shape, especially in the body around the neck.

DONKEY AND MULE (see pages 8 and 9)

The basic shape is the same as that for the pony, but the donkey's mane and tail are different. See the photograph. Also their ears are longer.

RABBIT (see page 28)

I have left the simplest one until last. It is made of a large white pom-pom body with two long knitted (or crocheted) ears.

The buildings (see Fig. 17)

As these can be knitted with any kind of yarn, from a fine 3-ply to thick rug-thrums, no specific instructions have been given regarding needles sizes, stitches or rows. Instead, each knitter should consult the chart and make the building-pieces to those measurements. It will be noted that extra buildings appear on some photographs; these have been made from the same patterns. Each building is filled with a block of foam cut to the correct shape. This should be made slightly larger than the knitting to ensure a snug fit. Extra instructions for each building, and materials, are given below.

SHED (see page 28)

This is the smallest of all the buildings. The walls are knitted in a simple k 1, p 2, rib pattern in dark brown, and the roof is worked in garter st. in rust.

BARN (see page 28)

This pattern is used also for the main part of the church, and for the stable-building seen on page 20. The barn is made of dark-brown yarn with beige/rust for the roof, which is knitted in garter st. The walls are knitted in k 1, p 2 rib. The walls of the other buildings are of stocking st., with a ridge around the base of 6 rows of garter st.

The barn-door is made in k 1, p 1 rib, decreasing at the top to make a curve. The edge is embroidered in chain st. to give a crisp finish.

CHURCH (see page 17 and back cover)

White yarn is used for the main part, and rust-mottled tweed for the roof, with oddments of dark and mid-brown.

FARMHOUSE (see pages 16 and 17)

Beige yarn is used for the walls, rust for the roof, and small amounts of other colours for windows and doors. The roof is knitted in double rib (k 2, p 2 on every row) and the walls begin with 6 rows of garter st., before continuing in stocking st.

The farmer tends his cows

The skewbald pony

The two children play with the rabbit

*The farmer cuts hay and the boy rakes it up. Their tools
lean against the shed*

RUG BASE (see Fig. 18)

Copy the diagram, full-scale, on to a large piece of brown paper, and use this as a pattern for the rug canvaswork. Place it underneath the canvas and draw on to this with a thick fibre pen. You will need rug canvas measuring 130cm. × 90cm., plus an extra 6cm. all round for turning under.

Yarns: thick knitting wools, rug-thrums and cut rug-wool will be most useful for the base, part of which is covered with tufting and some with stitchery (see Figs 19 and 20).

COLOURS AND STITCHES

Meadows: pale green 10cm. lengths of yarn knotted into the canvas as shown in the diagram.

Street and yard: grey/beige double-thickness yarn embroidered in tent st.

Ploughed fields: several different browns, knitted in single rib to the shapes of the pattern and sewn on to the canvas.

Cornfields: several different yellows, as follows:

Ripe corn: 18cm. lengths of double yarn in deep yellow, and knotted.

Cornfield 1: knotted with 16cm. lengths of deep green yarn, doubled.

Cornfield 2: two tones of green yarn, 20cm. long, knotted.

Cornfield 3: double yarn in tones of yellow and green, embroidered in tent st.

Cut corn: double yarn in tones of yellow, embroidered in satin st.

Hayfields and stubble: various light and medium greens used 4-fold in a wide satin st. for the Hayfield. The Stubble is worked in double yarn in tent st.

Bushes: deep green yarns, shown as shaded patches in the diagram. Short lengths of yarn are made into pom-pons and sewn onto the fields after these have been stitched.

Stream and pond: two or three different blues used together, embroidered in chain st.

The bridge is knitted in simple rib and stitched over the stream joining the street across the water.

TREES

You will need two tubes of cardboard for the inside of the trees; the tops are made of large pom-poms in thick, green yarn. The trunk is knitted as follows:

Using dark brown yarn on 3.5mm. needles, knit a piece measuring 14cm. long. Roll this around the cardboard tube and sew it up lengthways. Glue the pom-pom to the top. Each tree will stand more firmly if it is given a base of either tufted canvas or cardboard.

FLOWERS AND PLANTS

These can be knitted, crocheted, or made of tiny tufts of yarn from small oddments. They are extremely simple and can be made without a pattern; just crochet chains and link them together at a central point. These are scattered here and there around the scene, in front of the cottages, and around the trees and bushes.

RUCKSACK (see page 32)

Using 3-ply yarn and 2¼mm. needles, cast on 10sts and work in stocking st. for 24 rows.

Dec. 1st. at each end of the next 2 rows, then work 2 more rows. Cast off 6sts. The strap is a crochet chain, and the flap has an edge of crochet to keep it flat. It can be fastened with a press-stud.

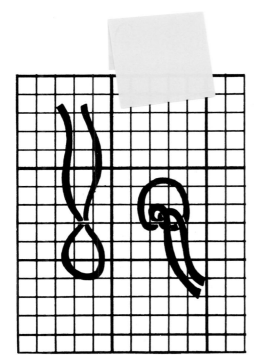

Fig. 19. Tufting on rug-canvas. This may be done without a tool; alternatively, with a crochet hook, or a latchet hook.

Fig. 20

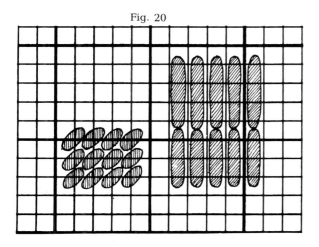

Fig. 20. Left: *Tent stitch.*
Right: *Satin stitch over three and four threads of the canvas.*

ACKNOWLEDGMENTS

The Knitted Farmyard

First published in Great Britain in 1985 by
Search Press Limited, Wellwood, North Farm Road,
Tunbridge Wells, Kent TN2 3DR

Tenth impression 1996.

First published in hardback in 2007
Reprinted 2008

Text by Hannelore Wernhard, translated by Hilary Simpson,
and edited by Jan Messent.

Original designs by Hannelore Wernhard; photographs by
Ulrike Schneiders; drawings by Jan Messent.

Hannelore Wernhard, Spiellandschaft © Christophorus im
Verlag Herder Freiburg im Breisgau 3rd edition 1987.

English version copyright © 1985 Search Press Ltd.

ISBN-13 978-1-84448-217-7
ISBN-10 1-84448-217-0

Printed in Malaysia

The family enjoys a picnic under the trees